ISBN 979-8-86-045121-6

INTRO

Welcome to our vibrant cookbook, where we celebrate the exciting world of Watertok. This trend has taken the internet by storm, turning the simple act of hydration into a fun, flavor-packed adventure.

Our cookbook is your passport to the world of Watertok, filled with recipes featuring syrups, packets, and infused water. These recipes are a blend of popular web and TikTok trends, and our own kitchen experiments. Whether you're a seasoned Watertok enthusiast or a curious newcomer, we've got a flavor journey waiting for you.

Our cookbook is divided into five exciting sections:
1. **Packet Power:** Flavoring water with packets only.
2. **Syrup Splash:** Flavoring water with syrup only.
3. **Mix Master:** Flavoring water by mixing syrups and packets.
4. **Natural Infusions:** Infusing water with fruits, herbs, and spices.
5. **Creative Corner:** Make your own recipes.

Remember, the beauty of Watertok lies in its versatility. Everyone's taste for flavored water is unique, so feel free to adjust the recipes to suit your own palate.

The real magic happens when you start experimenting. We encourage you to use our recipes as a starting point to create your own unique blends. To help you on this journey, we've included a handy table of compatible flavors and a special section for you to jot down your own recipes.

So, are you ready to ride the flavorful waves of Watertok? Grab a glass, pick a recipe, and let's dive in!

RATINGS

As you dive into our cookbook and try out these exciting recipes, we've got a fun little game for you. Why not rate your flavor experiences with our unique emoticon system?

Big Smile: "Flavor Fiesta!" - This is the ultimate accolade. If a recipe gets a Big Smile, it's a flavor sensation that sends your taste buds into a joyous jig!

Smile: "Tasty Treat!" - A recipe with a Smile is one that you really enjoyed. It's a delightful concoction that you'd happily sip on again.

Smirking Face: "Hmm, Interesting!" - A Smirking face means the recipe was okay. It didn't rock your world, but it had a certain something that piqued your interest.

Sad Face: "Oh, Bummer!" - If a recipe gets a Sad face, it means something didn't quite hit the mark. Maybe it was too sweet, too sour, or just a bit off balance.

Disgust: "Yikes, Not for Me!" - A Disgust face means the recipe wasn't to your liking at all. It's a flavor misstep that you'd rather not repeat.

Remember, these ratings are all in good fun and everyone's tastes are different. What's a "Yikes, Not for Me!" for you might be a "Flavor Fiesta!" for someone else. So, don't be shy about sharing your ratings!

HOW TO CREATE
PACKET POWER

Ready to transform your water into a flavorful treat? This section guides you through the delightful process of flavoring water using packets. These little packets are your ticket to a world of taste, transforming ordinary water into a flavorful treat.

1. **Use the Indicated Packets:** Each recipe in this book lovingly suggests a specific flavor packet. Let's start our journey there.
2. **Prepare Your Water:** Our recipes are crafted for 40 ounces of water, but your taste is unique! Feel free to adjust. As a general rule of thumb, one packet is perfect for 16 to 20 ounces of water.
3. **Add the Packets**: Now, the magic happens! Pour your chosen packet into the water.
4. **Mix It Up:** Stir until the powder dissolves, spreading the flavor evenly. It's like stirring a little potion of joy!
5. **Taste and Adjust:** Take a moment to savor your creation. If you'd like a stronger or milder flavor, feel free to add another packet or more water.

Remember, these packets are your creative tools. Mix different flavors, experiment, and most importantly, have fun! This is your journey, and we're here to guide you every step of the way.
Here's to a flavorful adventure!

Apple Cherry Jubilee

½ Pkt of Cherry

½ Pkt of Green Apple

Berry Apple Oasis

1 Pkt of Strawberry Kiwi

½ Pkt of Green Apple

BERRY BLAST

1 Pkt of Cherry

1 Pkt of Strawberry

AZURE CHERRY POM WHIRL

1 Pkt of Cherry Pomegranate

1/2 Pkt of Blueberry

Strawberry Melon Tango

1 Pkt of Watermelon

1 Pkt of Strawberry

Berry Tropical Swirl

1 Pkt of Mixed Berry

1/2 Pkt of Lime

1/2 Pkt of Mango

BLACKBERRY BURST

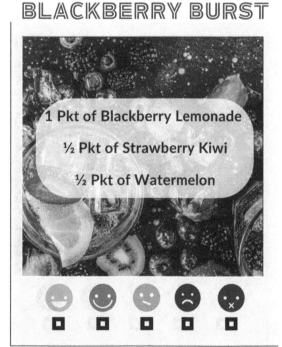

1 Pkt of Blackberry Lemonade

½ Pkt of Strawberry Kiwi

½ Pkt of Watermelon

BERRY LEMONADE

1 Pkt of Blue Raspberry

½ Pkt of Lemonade

Blueberry Grape Galore

1 Pkt of Blueberry

½ Pkt of Grape

Blueberry Bonanza

1 Pkt of Green Apple

1 Pkt of Blueberry

BERRY MELON MAGIC

1 Pkt of Melon

1/2 Pkt of Blueberry

BLUE HAWAII

2 Pkt of Blue Raspberry

½ Pkt of Cherry Limeade

½ Pkt of Pineapple

Caramel Apple Sip

1 Pkt of Green Apple

1/2 Pkt of Grape

1/2 Pkt of Cherry Limeade

Cactus Quencher

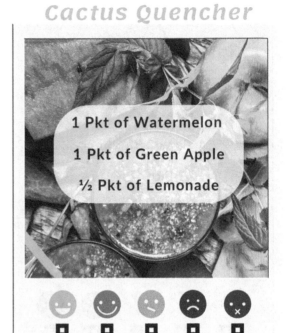

1 Pkt of Watermelon

1 Pkt of Green Apple

½ Pkt of Lemonade

BUBBLY BERRIES

1 Pkt of Grape

1 Pkt of Strawberry

CARIBBEAN SUNSHINE

1 Pkt of Cherry Limeade

1/2 Pkt of Pineapple

1 Pkt of Orange

Cherry Limeade Duo

1 Pkt of Cherry Limeade

1 Pkt of Cherry

Cherry Lime Typhoon

1 Pkt of Cherry Limeade

1 Pkt of Mixed Berry

CHERRY-BLUE WHIRL

1 Pkt of Blueberry

½ Pkt of Cherry

CHERRY OCEAN SPLASH

1 Pkt of Ocean Water

½ Pkt of Cherry

Citrus Mango Mingle

1 Pkt of Mango

1/2 Pkt of Orange

Citrus Orchard Zing

1 Pkt of Green Apple

1 Pkt of Lemon

CITRUS BERRY BURST

1 Pkt of Mixed Berry

1 Pkt of Orange

CITRUS SPLASH

1 Pkt of Orange

1 Pkt of Kiwi Lime

Fruit Fusion

1 Pkt of Lemonade

1 Pkt of Strawberry

½ Pkt of Tropical Punch

Golden Peach Paradise

1 Pkt of Pineapple

½ Pkt of Peach

FIESTA FRUIT PUNCH

1 Pkt of Margarita

½ Pkt of Tropical Punch

½ Pkt of Orange

DEEP BLUE SEA SPLASH

1 Pkt of Lemonade

1/2 Pkt of Blue Raspberry

½ Pkt of Tropical Punch

Holiday Hurrah

1 Pkt of Margaritaville Strawberry Daiquiri

1 Pkt of Skittles Tropical Kiwi Lime

½ Pkt of Lemonade

Kiwi Lime Berry Blast

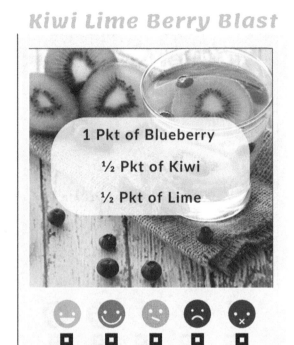

1 Pkt of Blueberry

½ Pkt of Kiwi

½ Pkt of Lime

GRAPE GALA

1 Pkt of Tropical Punch

1 Pkt of Grape

KIWI BERRY BLUES SYMPHONY

1 Pkt of Strawberry

½ Pkt of Blueberry

Mango Pineapple Magic

½ Pkt of Pineapple

½ Pkt of Mango

1/4 Pkt of Cherry

Lime Kissed Kiwi Berry Blend

1 Pkt of Strawberry Kiwi

1 Pkt of Lime

MANGO BERRY SPLASH

1 Pkt of Blueberry

1 Pkt of Orange

KIWI TYPHOON

1 Pkt of Mixed Berry

1 Pkt of Kiwi Lime

Melon Mango Medley

1 Pkt of Mango

1 Pkt of Watermelon

Orange Piney Passion

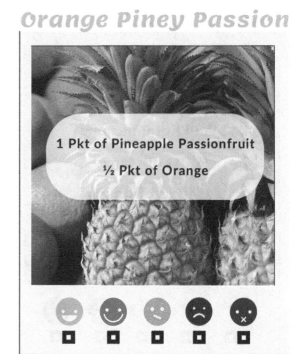

1 Pkt of Pineapple Passionfruit

½ Pkt of Orange

MYSTERY MIXER

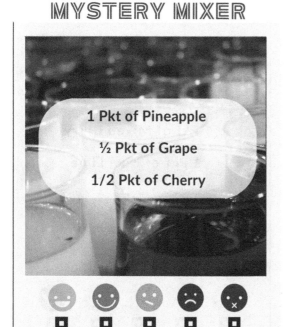

1 Pkt of Pineapple

½ Pkt of Grape

1/2 Pkt of Cherry

NERDS NEST

½ Pkt of Strawberry

½ Pkt of Blue Raspberry

Peach Berry Punch

1 Pkt of Cherry

½ Pkt of Peach

Peach Mango Magnifique

½ Pkt of Orange Peach Mango

½ Pkt of Mango

PEACHY BLUE FUSION

1 Pkt of Blueberry

½ Pkt of Peach

OCEAN BREEZE

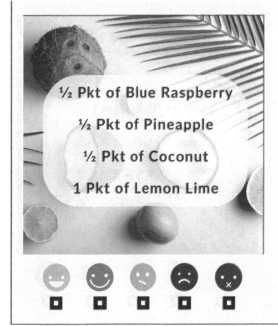

½ Pkt of Blue Raspberry

½ Pkt of Pineapple

½ Pkt of Coconut

1 Pkt of Lemon Lime

Pineapple Party

1 Pkt of Pineapple

½ Pkt of Fruit Punch

Pineapple Cherry Fiesta

1 Pkt of Cherry Pomegranate

1 Pkt of Pineapple

RASPBERRY APPLE RUSH

1 Pkt of Blue Raspberry

1 Pkt of Green Apple

PINK OCEAN SPLASH

1 Pkt of Ocean Water

½ Pkt of Strawberry

Sherbet Shimmer

½ Pkt of Kiwi Lime

1/2 Pkt of Mango

Raspberry Blastoff

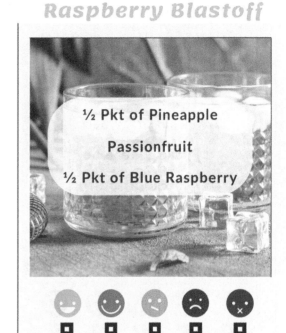

½ Pkt of Pineapple

Passionfruit

½ Pkt of Blue Raspberry

RUBY SUNRISE SERENADE

1 Pkt of Cherry Pomegranate

1/2 Pkt of Lemon

RED, WHITE & BLUE

1 Pkt of Blue Raspberry

1/2 Pkt of Cherry

Lime Juice To Taste

Strawberry Passionfruit Party

14 Pkt of Strawberry

1Pkt of Pineapple

Passionfruit

Spooky Sipper

1 Pkt of Tropical Punch

1 Pkt of Pineapple

Passion Fruit

STELLAR SIPS

1 Pkt of Green Apple

½ Pkt of Orange

½ Pkt of Pineapple

½ Pkt of Tropical Punch

SOUR BERRY WHIRLWIND

1 Pkt of Lemonade

1 Pkt of Mixed Berries

Content

Strawberry Pineapple Splash

½ Pkt of Strawberry

½ Pkt of Pineapple

Sun-Kissed Berry Bliss

1 Pkt of Strawberry

1 Pkt of Mango

SUN-KISSED PEACH DELIGHT

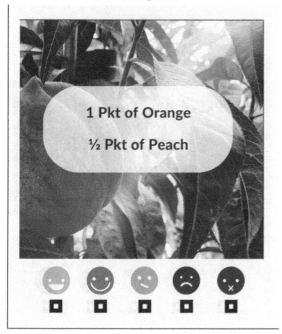

1 Pkt of Orange

½ Pkt of Peach

SUNRISE SPLASH

1 Pkt of Orange

1 Pkt of Pineapple

Sunset Berry Delight

1 Pkt of Blueberry

½ Pkt of Mango

Sunset Kiwi Samba

1 Pkt of Strawberry Kiwi

½ Pkt of Mango

SUNSHINE SIPPER

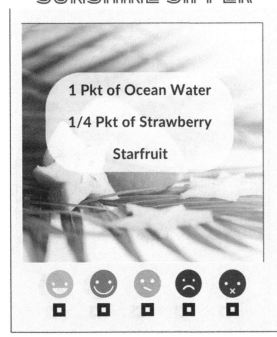

1 Pkt of Ocean Water

1/4 Pkt of Strawberry

Starfruit

TRIPLE TREAT

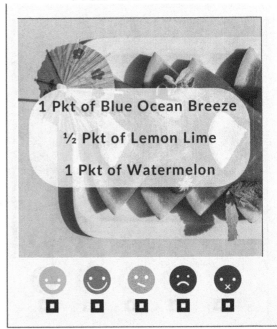

1 Pkt of Blue Ocean Breeze

½ Pkt of Lemon Lime

1 Pkt of Watermelon

Tropical Magic Elixir

1 Pkt of Passionfruit

½ Pkt of Orange

Tropical Lime Twist

1 Pkt of Mango

1/2 Pkt of Pomegranate

1/2 Pkt of Lime

TROPICAL RASPBERRY SUNSHINE

1 Pkt of Raspberry

1 Pkt of Mango

TROPICAL RUBY DREAM

1 Pkt of Cherry Pomegranate

1/2 Pkt of Mango

Tropical Tanglers

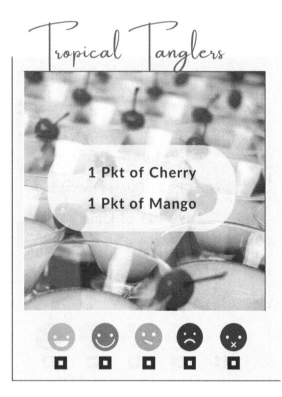

1 Pkt of Cherry

1 Pkt of Mango

Tropical Temptation

1Pkt of Tropical Punch

½ Pkt of Pineapple

½ Pkt of Fruit Punch

TWILIGHT KIWI BERRY DANCE

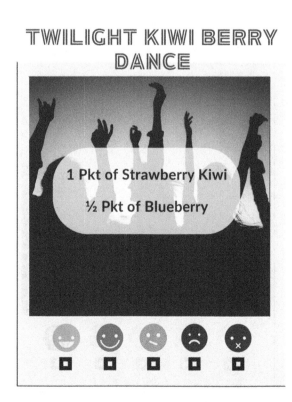

1 Pkt of Strawberry Kiwi

½ Pkt of Blueberry

TROPICAL TRANQUILITY

1 Pkt of Cucumber Limeade

½ Pkt of Blue Raspberry

Watermelon Berry Blast

½ Pkt of Watermelon

½ Pkt of Strawberry Starfruit

Vivid Zest Twirl

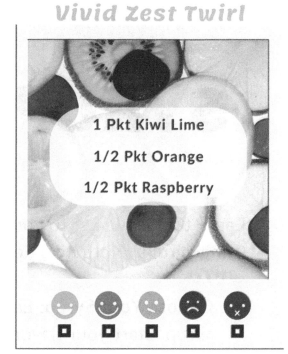

1 Pkt Kiwi Lime

1/2 Pkt Orange

1/2 Pkt Raspberry

WATERMELON WOW

½ Pkt of Pineapple

2 Pkt of Fruit Punch

½ Pkt of Watermelon

ZESTY MELON MIX

1 Pkt of Melon

1/2 Pkt of Lime

HOW TO CREATE
SYRUP SPLASH

Eager to add a twist to your water? This section is all about using syrups to create a delightful, flavorful beverage:

1. **Choose Your Syrup:** Each recipe suggests a specific syrup. Start your flavor journey with these recommendations.
2. **Add the Syrup:** Pour your chosen syrup into your water. We recommend starting with a small amount and adjusting to taste.
3. **Mix It Up:** Stir your water until the syrup is fully dissolved, creating a smooth and sweet blend.
4. **Taste and Adjust:** Savor your creation. If you'd like a stronger or milder flavor, feel free to adjust the amount of syrup or water.

Remember, this is your chance to experiment and have fun! Mix different syrups, adjust the quantities, and create your own sweet concoctions.

Happy flavoring!

Blushing Bride

1 Pump/1 Tbsp of Vanilla
Almond Syrup
½ Pump/½ Tbsp of
Strawberry Syrup
1 Pump/1 Tbsp of
Coconut Syrup

Ariel Daiquiri

1 Pump/1 Tbsp of Mermaid Syrup
1 Pump/1 Tbsp of Strawberry
Daiquiri Syrup

BUBBLEGUM BLISS

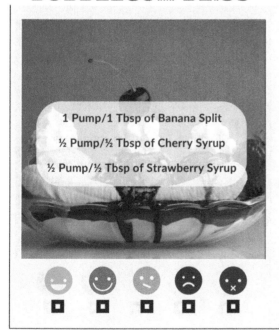

1 Pump/1 Tbsp of Banana Split
½ Pump/½ Tbsp of Cherry Syrup
½ Pump/½ Tbsp of Strawberry Syrup

AZURE BREEZE BLISS

1 Pump/1 Tbsp of Blueberry
Lavender Syrup
1 Pump/1 Tbsp of Pina Colada Syrup

Dragon Fruit Escape

1 Pump/1 Tbsp of Dragon Fruit Syrup

1 Pump/1 Tbsp of Pina Colada Syrup

½ Pump/½ Tbsp of Mermaid Syrup

Unicorn Magic

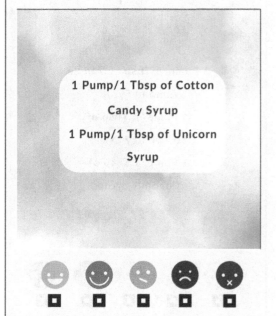

1 Pump/1 Tbsp of Cotton Candy Syrup

1 Pump/1 Tbsp of Unicorn Syrup

FRUIT SALAD

1 Pump/1 Tbsp of Strawberry Syrup

1 Pump/1 Tbsp of Coconut Syrup

ISLAND ESCAPE

1 Pump/1 Tbsp of Pineapple Syrup

1 Pump/1 Tbsp of Coconut Syrup

Strawberry Escape

1 Pump/1 Tbsp of Pina Colada Syrup

1 Pump/1 Tbsp of Mermaid Syrup

1 Pump/1 Tbsp of Strawberry Syrup

SILVER SIPPER

1 Pump/1 Tbsp of Vanilla Almond Syrup

SWEETLY EVER AFTER

1 Pump/1 Tbsp of Vanilla Almond Syrup

1 Pump/1 Tbsp of Coconut Syrup

VANILLA PEACH COAST

1 Pump/1 Tbsp of Vanilla Syrup

½ Pump/½ Tbsp of Peach Syrup

1 Pump/1 Tbsp of Coconut Syrup

HOW TO CREATE

MIX**MASTER**

Excited to blend syrups and packets for a unique taste experience? This section is where the magic really happens, as you create your own flavorful masterpiece:

1. **Choose Your Syrup and Packet:** Start with the recommended syrup and packet combination in each recipe.
2. **Add the Packet:** Pour your chosen packet into your water and stir until it's fully dissolved.
3. **Add the Syrup:** Now, add the syrup to your water. The syrup blends easily with the water, especially after the packet has been mixed in.
4. **Mix It Up:** Stir your water until both the syrup and packet are fully integrated.
5. **Taste and Adjust:** Savor your creation. Adjust the quantities of syrup, packet, or water to suit your taste.

Remember, this is your chance to experiment and have fun! Mix different syrups and packets, and create your own flavor combinations.

Happy flavoring!

Apple Rasberry Rush

1 Pkt of Blue Raspberry

½ Pkt of Green Apple

1 Pump/1 Tbsp of Candy

Apple Syrup

Banana Bonanza

1Pkt of Pineapple

1 Pump/1 Tbsp of Banana

½ Pump/Tbsp of Cherry Syrup

½ Pump/Tbsp of Strawberry Syrup

BANANA BREAK

1 Pump/1 Tbsp of Banana

1 Pkt of Pineapple

BERRY BANANZA DELIGHT

1 Pump/1 Tbsp of Banana

1 Pkt of Mixed Berry

Berry Bite

1 Pkt of Blue Raspberry

1 Pump/1 Tbsp of Raspberry Syrup

1 Pump/1 Tbsp of Cherry Syrup

Berry Cream Dream

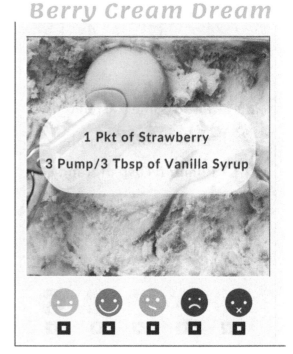

1 Pkt of Strawberry

3 Pump/3 Tbsp of Vanilla Syrup

BLISSFUL BERRY DREAM

1 Pkt of Strawberry

1 Pump/1 Tbsp of Raspberry Syrup

BLUE RAZZ REFRESHMENT

1 Pkt of Raspberry

2 Pumps/2 Tbsps of Coconut Syrup

Caramel Apple Quencher

1 Pkt of Green Apple

1 Pump/1 Tbsp of Salted

Caramel Syrup

Caramel Berry Rhapsody

1 Pump/1 Tbsp of

Caramel Syrup

1 Pkt Raspberry

CARAMEL COCONUT HARMONY

1 Pump/1 Tbsp of Caramel Syrup

1 Pkt Coconut

CHERRY COCONUT CRUISE

1 Pkt of Cherry

1 Pump/1 Tbsp of Coconut Syrup

Coconutty Concoction

1/2 Pkt of Strawberry

½ Pkt of Cherry

1Pump/1 Tbsp of Coconut Syrup

Citrus Daybreak

½ Pkt of Orange

1 Pkt of Pineapple

½ Pkt of Cherry Limeade

½ Pump/½ Tbsp of Coconut Syrup

½Pump/½ Tbsp of Vanilla Syrup

COCONUT BANANA COLADA

1 Pump/1 Tbsp of Banana

1 Pkt of Pineapple

1 Pump/1 Tbsp of Coconut Syrup

COCONUT CABANA

1 Pkt of Pineapple

2 Pumps/2 Tbsps of Coconut Syrup

Crimson Island Getaway

1 Pkt of Pineapple

½ Pkt of Cherry

1 Pump/1 Tbsp of Coconut

Syrup

Elderflower Citrus Pop

1 Pump/1 Tbsp of

Elderflower Syrup

1 Pkt Lime

ELDERFLOWER MANGO FIZZ

1 Pump/1 Tbsp of

Elderflower Syrup

1 Pkt Mango

ELDERBERRY BLOSSOM BLEND

1 Pump/1 Tbsp of

Elderflower Syrup

1 Pkt Blackberry

Elderflower Peach Margarita

1 Pump/1 Tbsp of
Elderflower Syrup
1 Pkt Peach
1/2 Pkt Lime

Green Mystery Mix

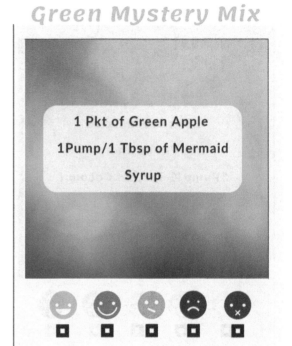

1 Pkt of Green Apple
1Pump/1 Tbsp of Mermaid
Syrup

ELDERFLOWER RASPBERRY RICKEY

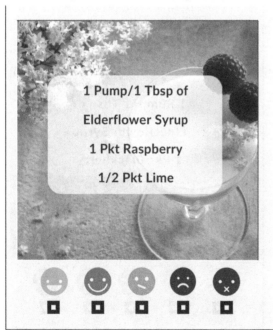

1 Pump/1 Tbsp of
Elderflower Syrup
1 Pkt Raspberry
1/2 Pkt Lime

GREEN APPLE SPLASH

1 Pkt of Green Apple
1 Pump/1 Tbsp of
Raspberry Syrup

Hibiscus Amber

1 Pump/1 Tbsp of Hibiscus Syrup

1 Pkt Orange

Hibiscus Apple Mirage

1 Pump/1 Tbsp of Hibiscus Syrup

1 Pump/1 Tbsp of Candy Apple Syrup

1 Pkt Orange

HIBISCUS MANGO CAROUSEL

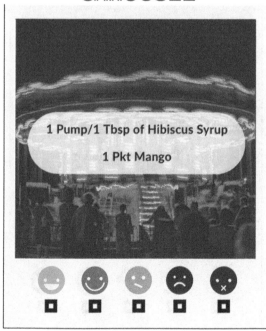

1 Pump/1 Tbsp of Hibiscus Syrup

1 Pkt Mango

GREEN OCEAN SPLASH

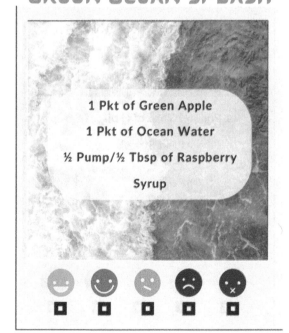

1 Pkt of Green Apple

1 Pkt of Ocean Water

½ Pump/½ Tbsp of Raspberry

Syrup

Hibiscus Beach Edition

1 Pump/1 Tbsp of Hibiscus Syrup

1/2 Pkt Lemonade

Hibiscus Lemonade Sparkle

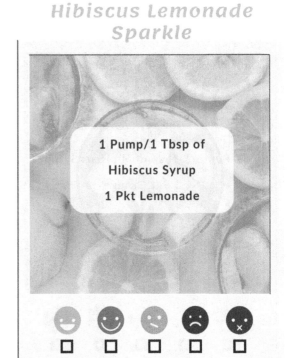

1 Pump/1 Tbsp of

Hibiscus Syrup

1 Pkt Lemonade

HIBISCUS BERRY FANTASY

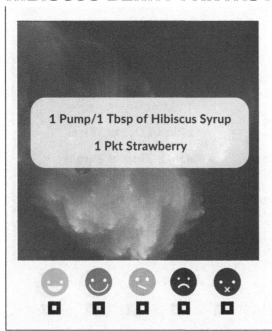

1 Pump/1 Tbsp of Hibiscus Syrup

1 Pkt Strawberry

HIBISCUS SUMMER DREAM

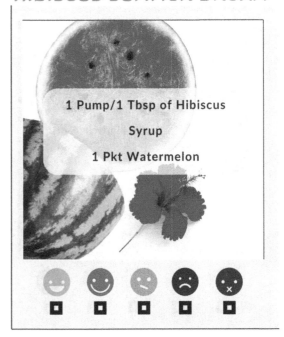

1 Pump/1 Tbsp of Hibiscus

Syrup

1 Pkt Watermelon

Hibiscus Whirl

1 Pump/1 Tbsp of Hibiscus

Syrup

1 Pkt Blueberry

Island Bliss

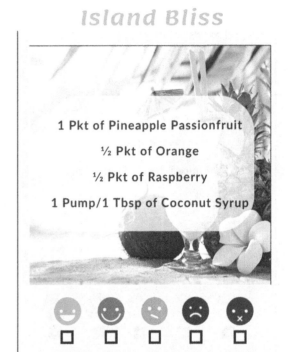

1 Pkt of Pineapple Passionfruit

½ Pkt of Orange

½ Pkt of Raspberry

1 Pump/1 Tbsp of Coconut Syrup

ISLAND BREEZE

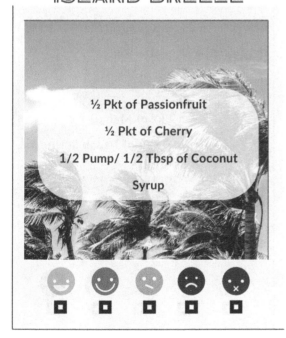

½ Pkt of Passionfruit

½ Pkt of Cherry

1/2 Pump/ 1/2 Tbsp of Coconut

Syrup

ISLAND FRUIT FIESTA

1/2 Pkt of Fruit Punch

½ Pkt of Mango

½ Pump/ 1/2 Tbsp of Coconut

Syrup

Kiwi Confection

1 Pkt of Kiwi Lime

1 Pump/1 Tbsp of Cake Syrup

Lemony Mermaid

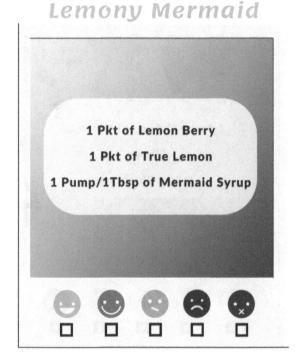

1 Pkt of Lemon Berry

1 Pkt of True Lemon

1 Pump/1Tbsp of Mermaid Syrup

MAGIC MIXER

1 Pkt of Wild Berry

1 Pump/1 Tbsp of Peach Syrup

1 Pump/1 Tbsp of Vanilla Syrup

MANGO MASHUP

1 Pkt of Mango

1 Pump/1 Tbsp of Peach Syrup

Mermaid Magic

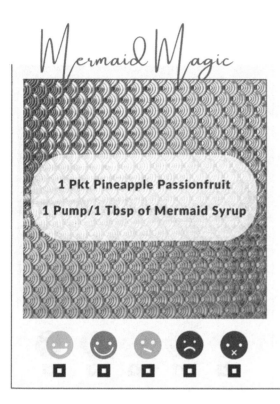

1 Pkt Pineapple Passionfruit

1 Pump/1 Tbsp of Mermaid Syrup

Mystical Citrus

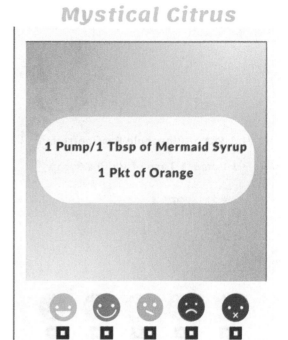

1 Pump/1 Tbsp of Mermaid Syrup

1 Pkt of Orange

MERMAIDS OF HAWAII

1Pkt of Mixed Berry

1 Pump/1 Tbsp of Mermaid Syrup

OCEAN AIR

1 Pkt of Blue Raspberry

1 Pump/1 Tbsp of Vanilla Syrup

1 Pkt of True Lemon

Passionfruit Punch

1 Pkt of Pineapple Passionfruit

1 Pump/1 Tbsp of Vanilla Syrup

Orange Creamsicle Quencher

1 Pkt of Orange

1 Pump/1 Tbsp of Vanilla Syrup

ORANGE FLOAT FIESTA

1 Pkt of Orange

1 Pump/1 Tbsp of Vanilla Syrup

2-4 Tbsps of Heavy Whipping Cream

Or Vanilla Creamer

PARADISE PUNCH

1 Pkt of Blue Raspberry

½ Pump/ ½ Tbsp of Peach Syrup

½ Pump/ ½ Tbsp of Mango Syrup

½ Pump/ ½ Tbsp of Coconut

Syrup

Peachy Mermaid

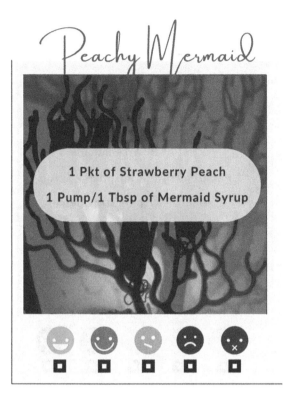

1 Pkt of Strawberry Peach

1 Pump/1 Tbsp of Mermaid Syrup

Pineapple Margarita Party

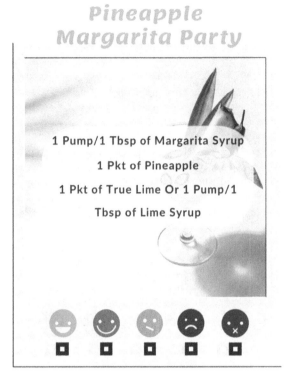

1 Pump/1 Tbsp of Margarita Syrup

1 Pkt of Pineapple

1 Pkt of True Lime Or 1 Pump/1

Tbsp of Lime Syrup

PINEAPPLE PUNCH

1 Pkt of Pineapple

1 Pump/1 Tbsp of Cherry Syrup

PINEAPPLE PERFECTION

1 Pkt of Pineapple

1 Pump/1 Tbsp of Vanilla

Syrup

Pink Perfection

½ Pkt of Strawberry

1 Pump/1 Tbsp of Lemon Syrup

Pink Lemonade

1 Pkt of Pink Lemonade

1 Pump/1 Tbsp of Raspberry Syrup

1 Pump/1 Tbsp of Strawberry Syrup

PINK PUNCH

1 Pkt of Cherry

1 Pump/1 Tbsp of Raspberry Syrup

PINK PARADISE

1 Pkt of Strawberry

1 Pkt of Dragon Fruit

1Pump/1 Tbsp of Coconut Syrup

*Dried Strawberries Optional

Pretty in Pink

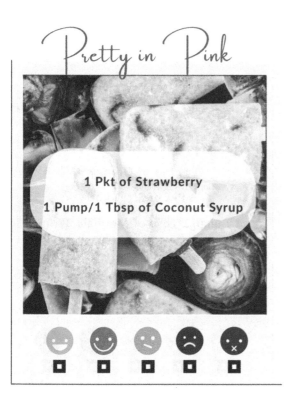

1 Pkt of Strawberry

1 Pump/1 Tbsp of Coconut Syrup

Strawberry Lemonade Luau

1 Pkt of Strawberry

1 Pkt of Pineapple

½ Pkt of Lemonade

1 Pump/1 Tbsp of Coconut Syrup

RASPBERRY WAVE

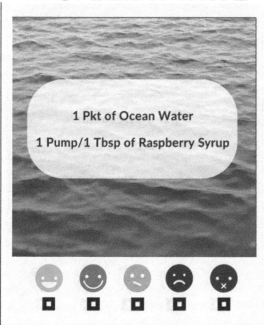

1 Pkt of Ocean Water

1 Pump/1 Tbsp of Raspberry Syrup

ROOT BEER FLOAT FEST

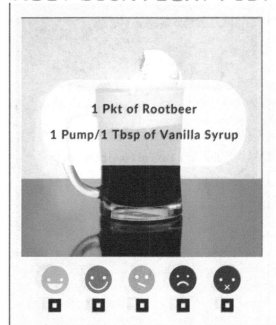

1 Pkt of Rootbeer

1 Pump/1 Tbsp of Vanilla Syrup

Sunset Sipper

1/2 Pkt of Cherry

½ Pkt of Mango

1 Pump/1 Tbsp of Strawberry Syrup

Sundown Serenade Mirage

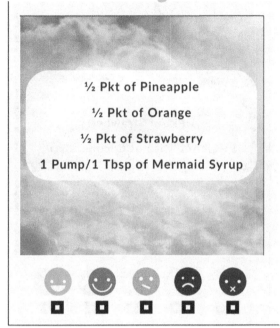

½ Pkt of Pineapple

½ Pkt of Orange

½ Pkt of Strawberry

1 Pump/1 Tbsp of Mermaid Syrup

SWEET SURPRISE

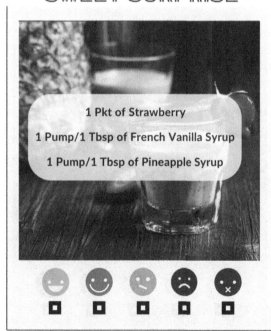

1 Pkt of Strawberry

1 Pump/1 Tbsp of French Vanilla Syrup

1 Pump/1 Tbsp of Pineapple Syrup

SWEET ORCHARD TWIST

1 Pkt of Green Apple

1 Pump/1 Tbsp of Caramel Syrup

Tangelo Twist

1 Pkt of Mango

1 Pump/1 Tbsp of

Raspberry Syrup

Tropical Melon Rhapsody

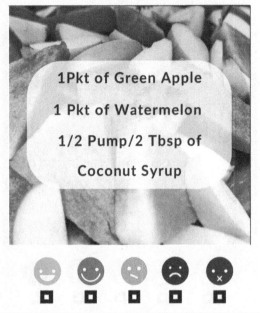

1Pkt of Green Apple

1 Pkt of Watermelon

1/2 Pump/2 Tbsp of

Coconut Syrup

TROPICAL PEACHY MONKEY TWIST

1 Pump/1 Tbsp of Banana

1 Pkt of Peach

1 Pkt of Lime

TROPICAL TREASURE FLIP

1 Pkt of Pineapple

1 Pump/1 Tbsp of Vanilla

Almond Syrup

Tropical Treats

½ Pkt of Strawberry

½ Pkt of Raspberry

1/2 Pump/2 Tbsp of
Coconut Syrup

Watermelon Fluff

1 Pump/1 Tbsp of Cotton
Candy Syrup

1 Pkt of Watermelon

WATERMELON WISHES

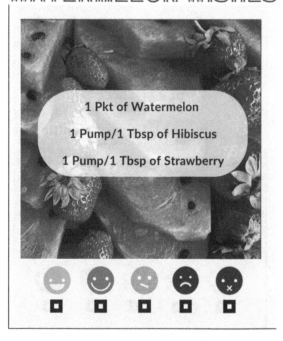

1 Pkt of Watermelon

1 Pump/1 Tbsp of Hibiscus

1 Pump/1 Tbsp of Strawberry

WATERMELON FLOWERS

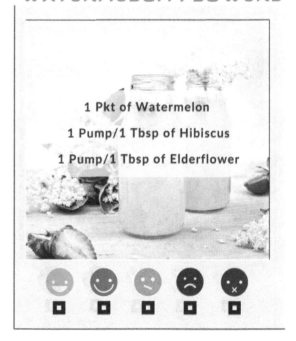

1 Pkt of Watermelon

1 Pump/1 Tbsp of Hibiscus

1 Pump/1 Tbsp of Elderflower

HOW TO CREATE
NATURAL INFUSION

Curious about a natural way to flavor your water? While not traditionally part of the Watertok trend, it's a delightful, natural method to add a flavor twist to your hydration routine.

1. **Select Your Ingredients:** Our recipes suggest specific fruits, herbs, or spices. Freshness is key for vibrant flavors!
2. **Prep Time:** Wash your ingredients. Slice fruits for more surface area, and lightly crush herbs to release their aromatic essence.
3. **Infusion Begins:** Add your ingredients to your water or an infuser. A gentle muddle can enhance flavor release.
4. **Patience Pays Off:** Let the water infuse for 2-4 hours at room temperature. For a deeper flavor profile, an overnight infusion in the refrigerator works wonders.
5. **Ready, Set, Serve:** If you used an infuser, just remove it. If not, strain the water. Your flavorful, infused water is ready to delight your taste buds!
6. **The Flavor Artist:** Enjoy your creation and let your imagination run wild. Experiment with different fruits, herbs, and spices to create your signature infusions.

Embark on this flavorful journey with us, exploring the natural and refreshing world of infused water!

Chia Fruit Fusion

1 Cup of Various Fresh

Fruits

1/8 Cup of of Chia Seeds

Cucumber Lemon Mint Symphony

1 Cucumber Thinly Sliced

1 Lemon Sliced

1/4 Cup of of Fresh Mint

BLACKBERRY CITRUS TWIST

½ Pint Blackberries

1 Orange Thinly Sliced

BLUEBERRY ORANGE BURST

1 Cup of Blueberries

1 Orange Sliced

Kiwi Blackberry Bliss

1 Kiwi Sliced

1/2 Pint Blackberries

Cucumber Mint Cooler

1 Thinly Sliced Cucumber,

1/4 Cup of Fresh Mint

(Muddled)

GRAPEFRUIT POMEGRANATE MINT MEDLEY

1 Grapefruit Thinly Sliced

1/2 Cup of Pomegranate Seeds

10 Fresh Mint Leaves

GINGER LIME ZEST

1 Piece Ginger Peeled And

Thinly Sliced

1 Lime Sliced

Lemon Zest

1 Sliced Lemon

Mango Raspberry Ginger Zest

1 Mango Peeled And Cubed

1/2 Pint Raspberries

1 (2-Inch) Piece Fresh Ginger

Peeled And Thinly Sliced

MELON MEDLEY

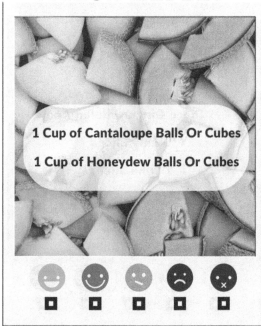

1 Cup of Cantaloupe Balls Or Cubes

1 Cup of Honeydew Balls Or Cubes

PINEAPPLE COCONUT LIME SPLASH

1 Cup of Pineapple Chunks

1 Cup of Coconut Chunks

1 Lime Thinly Sliced

Pomegranate Mint Refresh

1 Pomegranate In Pieces

1/4 Cup of Fresh Mint

Pineapple Orange Ginger Zest

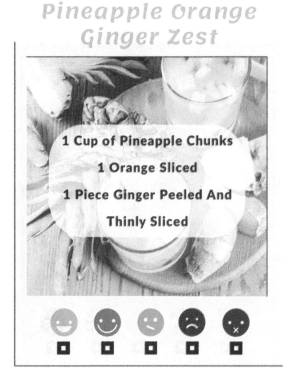

1 Cup of Pineapple Chunks

1 Orange Sliced

1 Piece Ginger Peeled And

Thinly Sliced

RASPBERRY ROSE VANILLA FUSION

1/2 Cup of Raspberries

1/4 Cup of Rose Petals

1 Vanilla Bean

RASPBERRY-ORANGE DELIGHT

1 Sliced Orange

1 Pint Raspberries

Strawberry Basil Delight

1/2 Cup of Strawberries Sliced

1/4 Cup of of Fresh Basil

Strawberry Lemon Zing

1/2 Fresh Strawberries

1 Lemon

TROPICAL PINEAPPLE TWIST

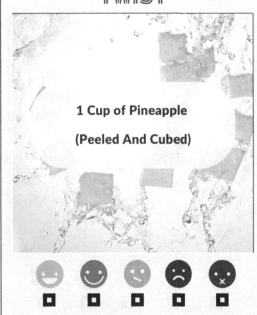

1 Cup of Pineapple

(Peeled And Cubed)

STRAWBERRY MANGO TANGO

1/2 Cup of Fresh Strawberries

1 Mango

Tomato-Basil Refresher

1 Cup of Cube Tomato

1/4 Cup of Fresh Basil (Muddled)

Strawberry-Cucumber Fusion

1 Thinly Sliced Cucumber

1 Cup of Quartered Strawberries

WATERMELON CUCUMBER SPLASH

1 Cup of Watermelon Cubes

1 Cucumber Thinly Sliced

WATERMELON KIWI LIME FUSION

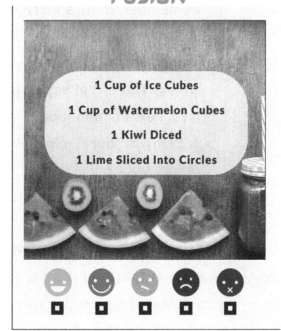

1 Cup of Ice Cubes

1 Cup of Watermelon Cubes

1 Kiwi Diced

1 Lime Sliced Into Circles

WELCOME TO THE
CREATIVE CORNER

Are you ready to embark on a culinary adventure? This part of our cookbook is your playground - a place to create your own recipes, explore new flavors, and discover delightful combinations:

1. **Discover the Flavor Charts:** We've provided two comprehensive flavor charts to inspire you. One chart outlines which fruits pair well together, and the other shows how fruits can be paired with non-fruit flavors. These guides are your stepping stones to flavor exploration.

2. **Select Your Ingredients:** Use the flavor charts as your compass, and select your ingredients. The world of fruits, herbs, spices, syrups, and packets is waiting for you.

3. **Create Your Own Combinations:** Now, let the fun begin! Mix and match different ingredients to create your own unique flavor medleys. Remember, there's no right or wrong here - it's all about what tantalizes your taste buds.

4. **Taste and Tweak:** Savor your creation. If it's not quite right, don't worry! You can always adjust the quantities, add more ingredients, or try a new combination.

5. **Jot Down Your Recipes:** We've included a special section for you to record your own recipes. This way, you can revisit your favorite combinations and recreate them whenever you want.

This is your flavor playground. It's a space for you to experiment, learn, and most importantly, enjoy. So, let your imagination run wild and create your own delicious flavored water recipes!

Here's to your flavorful adventure!

Flavor Pairing Guide
Fruit/Fruit

The rows and columns are labelled with the same list of fruits. A shaded (grey) cell marks the fruit paired with itself (the diagonal). A ">" mark indicates a recommended pairing between the row fruit and the column fruit. Columns are ordered left-to-right: Apple, Banana, Blueberry, Cherry, Coconut, Cranberry, Grapefruit, Huckleberry, Kiwi, Lemon, Lime, Lychee, Mango, Mixed Berry, Orange, Peach, Pear, Pineapple, Pomegranate, Rasberry, Strawberry, Tangerine, Watermelon, Yuzu.

Flavor Pairings	Apple	Banana	Blueberry	Cherry	Coconut	Cranberry	Grapefruit	Huckleberry	Kiwi	Lemon	Lime	Lychee	Mango	Mixed Berry	Orange	Peach	Pear	Pineapple	Pomegranate	Rasberry	Strawberry	Tangerine	Watermelon	Yuzu
Apple	▓	>	>	>		>		>		>							>				>			
Banana	>	▓	>	>	>											>								
Blueberry	>	>	▓	>				>		>						>					>			
Cherry	>	>	>	▓	>			>		>											>			
Coconut	>	>		>	▓							>	>	>	>		>	>	>	>	>	>	>	>
Cranberry		>				▓	>												>		>			
Grapefruit						>	▓			>												>		>
Huckleberry	>	>		>				▓	>									>			>			
Kiwi								>	▓	>			>					>			>			
Lemon	>		>	>			>		>	▓	>							>			>			>
Lime				>						>	▓	>						>			>			>
Lychee	>	>	>								>	▓	>	>	>				>		>			>
Mango	>	>	>						>			>	▓								>			
Mixed Berry	>	>	>	>								>		▓										
Orange												>			▓			>	>	>	>	>	>	
Peach		>													>	▓	>				>		>	
Pear		>															▓	>					>	
Pineapple	>															>	>	▓	>		>			
Pomegranate																			▓	>	>	>	>	>
Rasberry	>	>						>					>			>		>	>	▓	>	>	>	>
Strawberry	>	>	>	>																>	▓	>		>
Tangerine																						▓	>	
Watermelon		>		>	>		>		>	>	>	>	>	>	>	>	>	>	>	>	>	>	▓	>
Yuzu	>																				>		>	▓

55

Flavor Pairing Guide
Fruit/Non-Fruit

Flavor Pairings	Anise	Basil	Caramel	Chocolate	Cinnamon	Cola	Cucumber	Elderflower	Ginger	Hibiscus	Honey	Jalapeno	Lavender	Mint	Rose	Rosemary	Sage	Toffee	Thyme	Vanilla
Apple		✓	✓			✓		✓		✓		✓	✓		✓	✓	✓			✓
Banana		✓	✓			✓		✓		✓										✓
Blueberry					✓			✓		✓		✓			✓			✓		✓
Cherry			✓		✓			✓		✓										✓
Coconut			✓			✓		✓		✓						✓				✓
Cranberry		✓			✓			✓		✓		✓	✓		✓					✓
Grapefruit		✓						✓		✓		✓	✓	✓	✓	✓	✓			✓
Huckleberry								✓		✓										✓
Lemon	✓	✓						✓		✓	✓	✓	✓	✓	✓	✓	✓			✓
Lime	✓	✓			✓			✓		✓	✓	✓	✓	✓	✓	✓	✓		✓	✓
Lychee								✓		✓		✓	✓		✓					✓
Mango	✓	✓	✓		✓			✓		✓		✓	✓	✓	✓					✓
Mixed Berry	✓				✓			✓		✓		✓	✓		✓					✓
Orange	✓		✓		✓			✓		✓		✓	✓	✓	✓					✓
Peach	✓	✓	✓					✓		✓		✓	✓		✓			✓		✓
Pear	✓	✓	✓			✓		✓		✓		✓	✓	✓	✓			✓		✓
Pineapple	✓	✓						✓		✓		✓	✓		✓					✓
Pomegranate	✓		✓		✓			✓		✓		✓	✓	✓	✓	✓	✓			✓
Raspberry	✓	✓	✓		✓	✓		✓		✓		✓	✓	✓	✓	✓	✓	✓		✓
Strawberry	✓	✓	✓			✓		✓		✓		✓	✓	✓	✓	✓	✓	✓		✓
Tangerine	✓		✓		✓			✓		✓		✓	✓	✓	✓	✓	✓	✓		✓
Watermelon	✓	✓						✓		✓		✓	✓	✓	✓	✓	✓			✓
Yuzu	✓	✓						✓		✓		✓	✓		✓					✓

NAME: _____

NAME: _____

NAME: _____

NAME: _____

NAME: _____

NAME: _____

NAME: _____

NAME: _____

NAME: _____

NAME: _____

NAME: _____

NAME: _____

NAME: _____

NAME: _____

NAME: _____

NAME: _____

NAME: _____

NAME: _____

NAME: _____

NAME: _____

NAME: _____

NAME: _____

NAME: _____

NAME: _____

60

NAME: _____

NAME: _____

NAME: _____

NAME: _____

NAME: _____

NAME: _____

61

NAME: _____

NAME: _____

NAME: _____

NAME: _____

NAME: _____

NAME: _____

62

NAME: _____

NAME: _____

NAME: _____

NAME: _____

NAME: _____

NAME: _____

63

NAME: _____

NAME: _____

NAME: _____

NAME: _____

NAME: _____

NAME: _____

NAME: _____

NAME: _____

NAME: _____

NAME: _____

NAME: _____

NAME: _____

NAME: _____

NAME: _____

NAME: _____

NAME: _____

NAME: _____

NAME: _____

NAME: _____

NAME: _____

NAME: _____

NAME: _____

NAME: _____

NAME: _____

NAME: _____

NAME: _____

NAME: _____

NAME: _____

NAME: _____

NAME: _____

NAME: _____

NAME: _____

NAME: _____

NAME: _____

NAME: _____

NAME: _____

NAME: _____

NAME: _____

NAME: _____

NAME: _____

NAME: _____

NAME: _____

NAME: _____

NAME: _____

NAME: _____

NAME: _____

NAME: _____

NAME: _____

CONCLUSION

And there you have it, dear reader! You've journeyed with us through the exciting world of Watertok, exploring the delightful possibilities of flavoring water with syrups, packets, and infused water. You've discovered the joy of creating your own unique blends and the fun of rating your flavor experiences. Remember, the beauty of Watertok lies in its versatility and the endless possibilities it offers. Don't be afraid to experiment and adjust the recipes to suit your own palate. Use our handy table of compatible flavors as a guide, but feel free to venture off the beaten path and create your own flavor combinations.

As you continue your Watertok journey, we hope you'll find joy in the simple act of hydration. We hope you'll see each glass of water not just as a necessity, but as an opportunity to explore, create, and enjoy.

Thank you for joining us on this flavorful adventure. We can't wait to see where your Watertok journey takes you next. Remember to have fun, stay hydrated, and keep exploring the wonderful world of flavors!

Made in the USA
Las Vegas, NV
08 December 2023

82338120R00044